For more information about Troll Mountain, visit
www.trollmountainstory.com

ISBN: 978-0-9861272-3-6

Mike Eats the Cheese

Written by Dan Schieberl
Illustrated by Brett Grunig

Mike Eats the Cheese

A Troll Mountain Story

Written by Dan Schieberl

Illustrated by Brett Grunig

To Bram.

A special thanks to Anne Jordan for her
wit, wisdom and love of writing.

There is a special harvest celebration in Troll Village, with lots of fun contests. Gädd, the Village Elder, has a dilemma. "Where is Mike, the Drag-Rex?" he asks his grandson, Avarr. "Have you seen Mike? He is supposed to be helping Ragnar with the cheese contest."
"You know how a Drag-Rex can be, Grandpa," explains Avarr. "They get distracted so easily."

"I refuse to cut any more cheese,"
Ragnar stands in protest. "It's stinky!
This is Mike's job. Where is he?"

"Oh my!" exclaims Gädd. "Who is going to help us prepare for the cheese contest?" Avarr declares, "I'll find Mike!" and takes off running.

Avarr stops at the first contest, which is the balance beam, and sees Helga inching across a log suspended over a mud pit.

"Helga, have you seen Mike? We need his help in the cheese booth. Can you help me look for him?"

"Sure! I'd love to help." Suddenly, Helga slips and falls into the mud pit. She's covered head to toe in mud. Avarr sighs, "I guess you can't help now." "Sorry, Avarr!" says Helga dripping in mud.

Next, Avarr sprints over to
the cherry-pit spitting contest
where his friend, a large bear
named Yukon, is the judge.

A pair of conjoined teenage troll twins, Ramm and Bramm, stand at the front of the line. They each toss a cherry into their mouths. "You're next, Ramm and Bramm. Ready?" Yukon asks the twins. They eagerly nod, "Yes." The first one, Bramm puckers up his lips and spits the cherry pit a very long distance. Yukon takes his flag and marks the spot where Bramm's pit falls. "Well done, Bramm. That's a new record!" exclaims Yukon.
He turns to Ramm and says, "You're next!"

Ramm and Bramm twist around. Now Ramm is ready to take aim. Determined to outdo his brother, Ramm takes a deep, deep breath and . . . gulp . . . he swallows the cherry pit!

Yukon takes a flag and marks the spot where Ramm stands.

"Hey Yukon, I need to find Mike, can you help?" asks Avarr. "Sorry, Avarr," says Yukon, apologetically. "I'm busy with the cherry-pit spitting contest."

Avarr rushes over to the Swing Tree.
There's Mike The Drag-Rex!
He is occupied helping the village mothers entertain
their troll children on the swings.
He uses his powerful tail to push them.

One troll child screams, "Higher, Mike! I want to go higher!" Mike glances deviously over his shoulder. When he sees that the mothers are busy, he swooshes his big tail and sends the swing flying high into the air.

The troll child becomes completely wrapped around the tree branch! He screams in glee, "Do it again, Mike! Do it again!"

The mothers glance over at the child and cry out when they
see that he's stranded in his swing. They yell, "You can't do that, Mike!"
Mike looks sheepishly at the ground. A young child declares,
"Look! Mike's Mood Mane changed to blue!"

Avarr helps his friend Mike get out of the uncomfortable situation. "Come with me, Mike," Avarr says. "You've gotten distracted again. You have a job to do."

"The cheese booth!" Mike exclaims.
"I completeley lost track of time again! How could I forget? Cheese is my favorite!"
Mike licks his chops just thinking of cheese.

Mike The Drag-Rex loves nothing more than CHEESE. He loves Gouda and Swiss, Muenster and Brie, Cheddar and Mozzarella, Monterey Jack and Provolone. He likes hard cheese, soft cheese, cheese with holes in it, and even stinky cheese. Mike doesn't care what kind of cheese it is - whether it's white cheese, yellow cheese, brown cheese or even blue cheese! Mike loves cheese. He is going to be the perfect helper at the cheese booth.

Inside the cheese booth, Mike is slicing the cheese into perfectly square cubes. He cuts two pieces, puts one onto a tray and then pops one into his mouth. Hiding behind a barrel, Ramm and Bramm watch in amazement as Mike eats half of the cheese, one piece at a time.

Ramm turns to Bramm and whispers, "Let's play a joke on Mike."
Bramm nods eagerly. "Yeah, let's do it!"

"Let's hide the cheese from Mike and make him think he ate it all," says Ramm.
"What a great idea," says Bramm, "I'm so glad I thought of it."
"What? No you didn't."
"Now's not the time to argue about minor details," says Bramm as he peaks around the barrel.

Mike sings to himself as he
continues to cut the cheese.
"One for the contest, one for
me. I'm such a good Drag-Rex,
I deserve three." Mike pops
three pieces of cheese
into his mouth.

He looks down at the cheese board and sees that he has finished cutting all the cheese. Mike then looks at the cheese platter and sees that it is also empty.

Avarr and Gädd come over to the cheese booth to check on Mike. As the time nears for the cheese contest, a crowd gathers in front of the booth. "I'm sorry, Avarr. I'm sorry, Gädd, but I ate all the cheese," Mike apologizes.

The crowd gasps. A woman yells out, "Punish him!" More people join in the chant, "Punish the Drag-Rex!"

Behind the barrel, Ramm and
Bramm giggle as they watch
Mike squirm before the crowd.
Gädd hears their giggles.
He goes around to the back of
the cheese booth and sneaks up
on Ramm and Bramm. Gädd sees
the tray of cheese cubes. "Oh, ho!
What do we have here?"
grumbles Gädd. The twin
brothers gulp.

"We were just having some fun!"
"You can't have fun at someone else's expense. That's not a nice thing to do," explains Gädd as he drags the twins back to the booth. He hands the tray of cheese to Mike.

"You didn't eat all the cheese, Mike. Ramm and Bramm were playing a mean trick on you." Mike faces Ramm and Bramm. "You were going to let me get into trouble?"

"It was a joke! It's funny, right?" Ramm asks.
"I think it's funny!" The twins start to laugh.
The crowd in front of the cheese booth demands
justice for Mike. "Punish them! Punish those trickster twins."
Gädd smiles. "I've got just the lesson for these two."

Mike watches as Ramm and Bramm sit on a stool in the pie-throwing contest. The troll villagers line up to throw pies at the twins. Splat! A blackberry pie hits Ramm in the face. The villagers laugh. "Now, that's funny!"

"Your turn, Bramm," says Ramm. "No, no that's okay. I'll let you do it." "It's blackberry pie!" says Ramm.

Bramm immediately twists around and gets hit with a rhubarb pie. "That's definitely not blackberry!" Bramm coughs. Ramm laughs.

Back at the cheese booth, Gädd boasts, "Avarr, you saved the day, you found our judge!" Mike holds a one-person cheese contest. He pops different cheeses into his mouth. "Hmm, the Gouda is perfect." Mike pops another cube of cheese into his mouth and exclaims, "But this Mozzarella is the best!" Gädd smiles and declares, "This cheese contest is officially over. Mozzarella is the winner!"

THE END